La Bohème
Vocal Score

Giacomo Puccini

DOVER PUBLICATIONS, INC.
Mineola, New York

La Bohème in Full Score is available
in Dover edition 0-486-25477-1

Bibliographical Note

This Dover edition, first published in 2000, is a republication of an author-
itative early edition. Lists of credits and contents are newly added.

International Standard Book Number: 0-486-41386-1

Manufactured in the United States of America
Dover Publications, Inc., 31 East 2nd Street, Mineola, N.Y. 11501

LA BOHÈME

Opera in Four Acts

Music by Giacomo Puccini

Libretto by Giuseppe Giacosa and Luigi Illica,
based on Henri Murger's novel *Scènes de la vie de Bohème* (1847–9).
English version of Acts I and II by William Grist and Percy Pinkerton;
Acts III and IV by Percy Pinkerton. Piano reduction by Carlo Carignani.

First performance
1 February 1896, Teatro Regio, Turin
Arturo Toscanini conducting

CHARACTERS

Mimì	Soprano
Musetta	Soprano
Rodolfo, *a poet*	Tenor
Marcello, *a painter*	Baritone
Schaunard, *a musician*	Baritone
Colline, *a philosopher*	Bass
Parpignol, *a toyseller*	Tenor
Bénoit, *a landlord*	Bass
Alcindoro, *a Councillor of State*	Bass
A Sergeant of the Customs Office	Bass
A Customs Officer	Bass

Students, shopkeepers and street hawkers,
café waiters and street sweepers, soldiers,
men, women and children of the town

Setting: Paris, about 1830

CONTENTS

LA BOHÈME

BY
GIACOMO PUCCINI

FIRST ACT

IN THE ATTIC

Spacious window from which one sees an expanse of snow - clad roofs, on left a fireplace. A table, a small cupboard, a little book - case, four chairs, a picture easel, a bed; a few books, many packs of cards, two candle-sticks. Door in the middle; another on left.

(Curtain rises quickly. Rudolph and Marcel - Rudolph looks pensively out of the window, Marcel works at his painting "The Passage of the Red Sea" with hands nipped with

cold, and warms them by blowing on them from time to time, often changing position, on account of

the frost.)

4

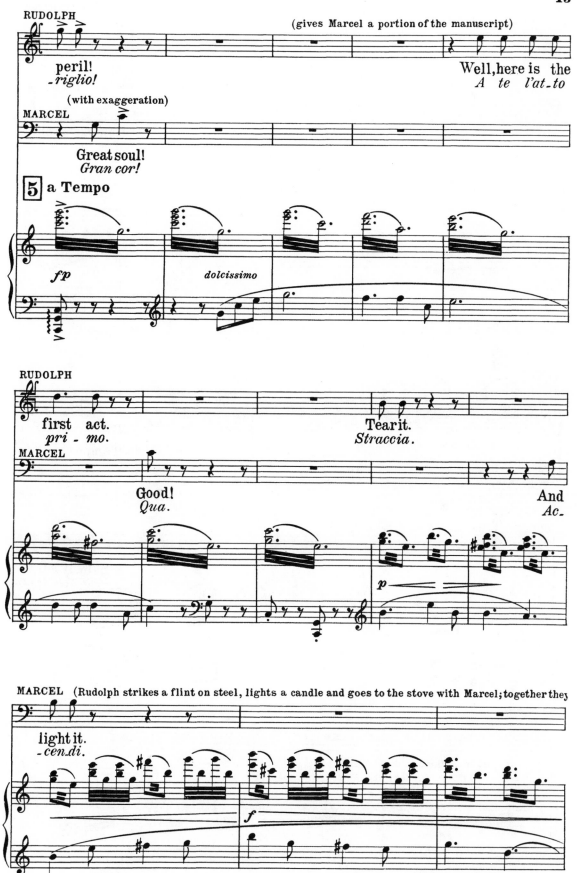

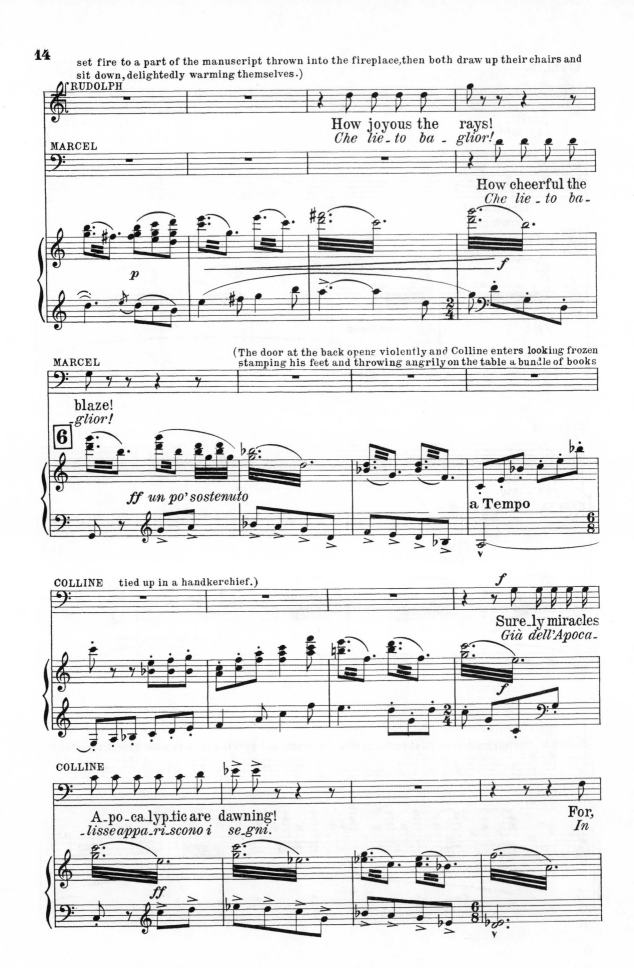

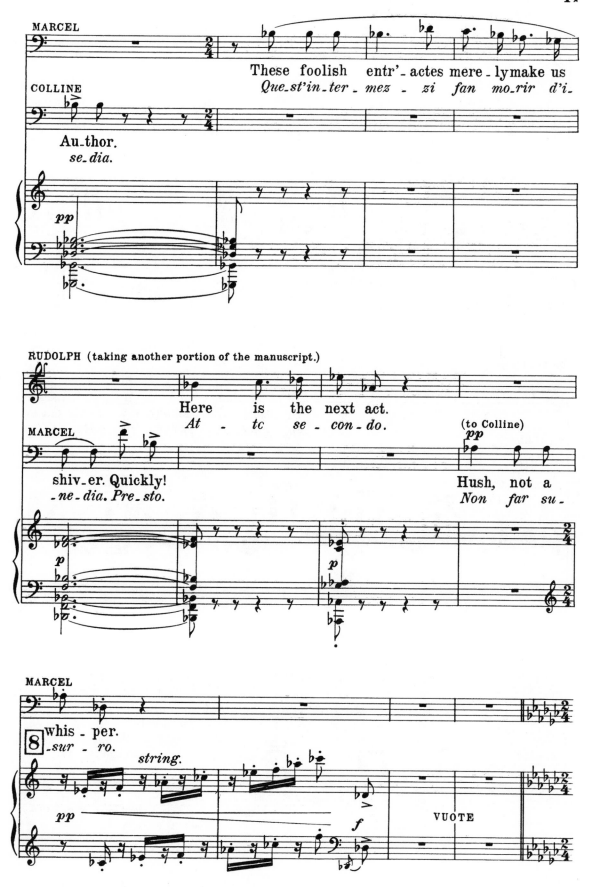

(Rudolph tears up the manuscript and throws it on the fireplace, the flame revives. Colline moves his chair nearer and warms his hands, Rudolph is standing near the two with the rest of the manuscript.)

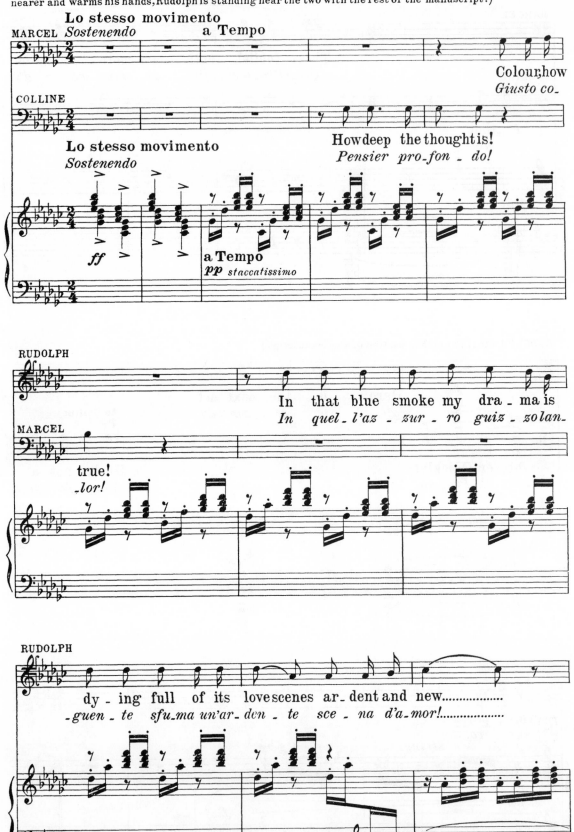

(From the middle door enter two boys, one bearing food, wine and cigars, the other a faggot of wood. At the noise, the three at the fire turn round, and with a cry of wonder they dart on the provisions borne by the boys and deposit them on the table; Colline takes the wood and carries it near the stove.)

24

(seeing that no one is listening, grasps Colline as he passes with a plate)

SCHAUNARD

parsley gulps, as So-crates is dead..................... The de-vil fly a-
_ze_mo_lo, da So_crate mo_ri!..................... Che il dia_vo_lo vi

COLLINE

parlato

Who?
Chi?

SCHAUNARD *Opp.*

(seeing the rest in the act of commencing to eat the cold pie.)
Poco meno

_way with you en_tire_ _ _ly. What are you
por_ti tut_ti quan_ _ _ti! Ed or che

leggero 3
Poco meno

SCHAUNARD *gridato*

(with solemn gesture extends his hand over the pie and prevents
his friends from eating it, then takes the eatables from the table,

do_ _ing? No! dain_ties of this kind Are but the stored_up
fa_ _te? No! Que_ste ci_ba_rie so_no la sal_me_

and puts them in the cupboard) *rall:*..................... *a piacere*

SCHAUNARD

fod_ _der saved for the morrow. Fraught with gloom and sor_row: To dine at
_ri_ _a pei dì fu_tu_ri te_ne_bro_sie o_scu_ri. Pranzare in

32

46

48

(takes a light from the table and goes to open the door; Marcel, Colline and Schaunard go out and descend the staircase.)

RUDOLPH

Five minutes on _ ly
Cin _ que mi _ nu _ ti.

MARCEL

De _ lay and you'll hear the chorus.
Se tar _ di,u _ drai che co _ ro!

COLLINE

at the porter's lodge.
_ bas _ so dal por _ tier.

SCHAUNARD (leaving)

You must cut short the Beaver's growing tale!
Ta _ glia cor _ ta la co _ da al tuo Ca _ stor!

Allegro vivo.(I.tempo)

24 Allegro vivo.(I.tempo)

pp

MARCEL

(from without)

Look to the stair _ case;
Occhio al _ la sca _ la.

RUDOLPH .... a Tempo

list-en, pretty maiden, while I tell you in a mo_ment Just who I
-spet_ti si-gno-ri_na, le di-rò con due pa-ro-le chi son, chi

RUDOLPH

am, What I do, and how I live.....................
son, e che fac-cio, co-me vi-

(Mimi is silent; Rudolph lets go her
hand, when recoiling she finds a
chair, into which she drops as if
overcome by emotion)

RUDOLPH   rall:.....................

.... Shall   I?   I
-vo.   Vuo -   - le?   Chi

RUDOLPH
Andante sostenuto

am,   I am,   I am a po_et. What's my em_
son?   chi son? Sono un po-e-ta. Che co-sa

RUDOLPH

_ployment?   Writ_ing!   Is that a   liv_ing?   Hardly!
fac_cio?   Scri_ vo.   E co_me   vi_vo?   Vi_vo.

RUDOLPH

Andante lento ♩=52

I've wit tho' wealth be wanting; Ladies of rank   and
In po_ver_tà   mia lie_ta   scia_lo da gran si_

32

dolce   **Andante lento** ♩=52

RUDOLPH

fashion... all inspire me with passion, In dreams and fond ill _us_ ions or castles in the
_gno_re....rime ed in _ni d'a_mo_re. Per so_gni e per chi_me_re   e per castelli in

RUDOLPH

allarg.   rit.
con molta espress.

air..........   Richer is none on earth   than I!   Bright
a_ria....   l'_anima ho mi_lio_na_   _ria.   Ta_

MIMI

fan _ cies and of vi _ sions bright they tell me,............... such as
par _ la _ no di so _ gni e di chi _ me _ re,............... quel _ le

MIMI

a Tempo

po _ ets, and on _ ly po _ ets know, Do you hear me?
co _ se che han nome po _ e _ si _ a... Lei m'in _ ten _ de?

RUDOLPH

(moved)

a Tempo

Yes.
Sì.

rall:.................................. rall:..................................

MIMI Lentamente

They call me Mi _ mi, But I know not why!
Mi chiama _ no Mi _ mì, il per _ chè non so.

Lentamente

molto espressivo   pp   pp   pp

Allegretto moderato ♩ = 144

MIMI con semplicità

All by my _ self I take my frugal sup _ per; To mass not oft re _
So _ la, mi fo il pran _ zo da me stes _ sa. Non va _ do sempre a

37

Allegretto moderato ♩ = 144

p

MIMI *con grande espansione* *allarg.*

Spring's first sweet fra-grant kiss is mine!............... is
il pri - mo ba - cio del-l'a - pri - le è

f *allarg.*

MIMI *a Tempo* *con espressione intensa* *rall.molto*.....................

mine!............... Her first bright sun - beam is
mi - o!........ il pri - mo so - le è

dim. *pp* *a Tempo* *rall.molto*..................

MIMI **I.Tempo andante** *agitando appena* *Sostenendo*

mine! A rose, as her pe - tals are ope-ning, Do I tenderly
mi - o!... Ger-moglia in un va-so u-na ro - sa... Foglia a foglia la

I.Tempo andante *agitando appena*

pp *Sostenendo*

MIMI *allarg.* *ten.*

cher - ish. Ah!What a charm lies for me in her
spi - o! Co - sì gen - til il pro-fu - mo d'un

allarg. *col canto*

p

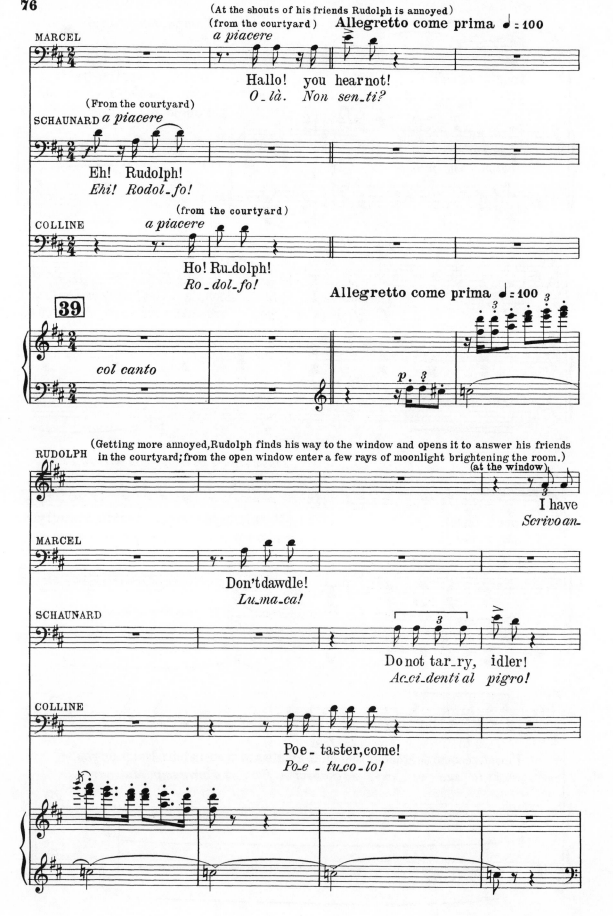

78

(Mimi goes still nearer to the window, so that the moon's rays fall upon her)

End of Act.I.

SECOND
ACT

SECOND ACT

IN THE LATIN QUARTER

A conflux of streets; where they meet, a square flanked by shops of all sorts; on one side, the Café Momus.

CHRISTMAS EVE

A vast, motley crowd; soldiers, serving-maids; boys, girls, children, students, work girls, gendarmes etc. etc. Outside their shops vendors are bawling, inviting purchasers. Aloof from the crowd, Rudolph and Mimi walk up and down; Colline is near a rag shop. Schaunard stands outside a tinker's buying a pipe and a horn. Marcel is being hustled hither and thither. Sundry townsfolk are seated at a table outside the Café Momus. It is evening. The shops are decked with tiny lamps; a huge lantern lights up the entrance to the Café.

88

Hot roasted chest_nuts. Trinkets and cros_ses, Fine hard _ bake!..........
Cal _ di i mar _ ro _ ni. Nin _ no _ li, cro _ ci. Tor _ ro _ ni!.............

Hot roasted chest_nuts. Trinkets and cros_ses, Fine hard _ bake!..........
Cal _ di i mar _ ro _ ni. Nin _ no _ li, cro _ ci. Tor _ ro _ ni!.............

Ah!........................
Ah!........................

a   rack _ _ _ _ et!   What up_roar!
_ta   fol _ _ _ la!   Che chias_so!

Hot roasted chest_nuts!   ex _ cellent tof_fee and hardbake!
Cal _ di i mar _ ro _ ni   e   ca_ra_mel _ le. Tor _ ro _ ni!

HAWKERS

.... Cream   foam _ ing and froth _ y!.................
.... *Pan _ na .... mon _ ta _ ta!.................*

.... Fine   hard _ bake! Fine hard _ bake!.................
.... *Oh!   la .... cro _ sta _ ta!.................*

(Curtain rises)

94

(a group of sales women enter)

MARCEL (the girl runs away, laughing)

Who'll give a penny for my virgin heart?
Io dò ad un soldo il ver-gi-ne mio cuor!

SCHAUNARD (strolls about in front of the Café Momus waiting for friends; and armed with his huge pipe and hunting-horn, he intently watches the crowd.)

Surging onward, ea _ ger, breathless, moves the madding
Fra spin_to_ni e pe _ sta _ te ac _ cor _ ren_do af-

Sop. 1i

SALESWOMEN

Buy our pret_ty scarf_pins! Try our tof_fee and our
Nin _ no_li, spil _ let _ te! Dat _ te_ri e ca _ ra _ _

Sop. 2i

Buy our pret_ty scarf_pins! Try our tof_fee and our
Nin _ no_li, spil _ let _ te! Dat _ te_ri e ca _ ra_ _

SCHAUNARD

throng, as they fro_lic, fro_lic, ev _ er in their wild and
_fret _ ta la fol_la e si di _ let _ ta nel pro_var gio_ie

5

P leggero

(Marcel, Schaunard and Colline try to find an empty table outside the Café; but there is only one, which is occupied by townsfolk. At these latter the three friends glare furiously, and then enter the Café)

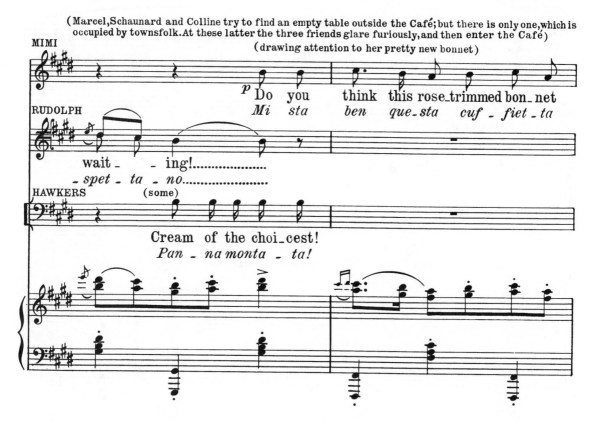

(At a shop in the rear, a shopman, gesticulating frantically, stands on a stool and offers underclo_
thing, nightcaps etc. for sale. Boys in a group surround his shop, and gaily burst out laughing)

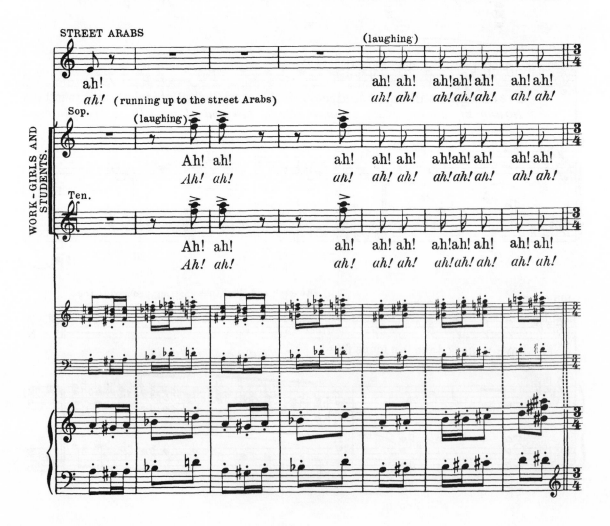

Let's get a way, I'm cho _ king!
Io sof _ fo _ co, par _ tia _ mo!

near _ est!
_ ri _ no!

The coff _ ee's com _ ing
Ve _ di, il caf _ fe è vi _

Cream from the dai _ ry!
Pan _ na mon _ ta _ ta!

Bassi 1!

Flowers for the la _ dies!
Fio _ ri al _ le bel _ le!

cres. sempre

(they enter the café)

(from all sides folk flock to the square; by degrees
the crowd collects at the back of the stage.)

Let's go to the "Mo _ mus!"
An _ diam là da Mo _ mus!

now! Let's go to the "Mo _ mus!"
_ cin! An _ diam là da Mo _ mus!

O _ ranges, ap _ ples and chest _ nuts all hot!
Nin _ no _ li, dat _ te _ ri, cal _ di mar _ ron!

Bassi 1!

O _ ranges, choc _ o _ late, hardbake and
A _ ranci, dat _ te _ ri, nin _ no _ li,

Bassi 2!

Chaf _ finches, or _ tolans, jun _ ket, what
Frin _ guelli, pas _ se _ ri, pan _ na, tor _

(To the waiter who hurries back into the café while another comes out to lay the table.)

(Rudolph and Mimi reach the café.)

RUDOLPH

Allᵗᵗᵒ moderato ♩.=76

come. This is Mi — mi, the mer-ry flow'r girl, And
qui. *Questa è Mi — mì, ga-ia fio-ra-ia. Il*

10

RUDOLPH

now she's come to join us, Our par-ty is com-ple-ted,......
suo ve-nir com-ple-ta la bel-la com-pa-gni-a,........

RUDOLPH

rit:............................

.... for I,..................... for I shall play the po — et,
.... *per-chè..................... per-chè son io il po-e — ta;*

cres. *f*

RUDOLPH

espansivo

a Tempo

While she's the muse in-car — nate............ Forth from my
es-sa la po-e-si — a................ Dal mio cer-

rall:............................... *pp* **a Tempo**

112

(Enter Parpignol from the Rue Dauphin, pushing a barrow festooned with foliage, flowers and paper lanterns. He is surrounded by a crowd of merry urchins.)

(Urchins in a group wrangle round the bar-
-row, while their scolding mothers approach,

gun, and I the whip,
- non, voglio il fru - stin,

Get away! they are mine.
dei sol-da-ti i drap-pel.

MARCEL
(looking at the menu

I'll have
Un tac-

SCHAUNARD

Bring some venison!
Cer-vo ar - ro-sto!

but their threats of punishment prove futile, for the children refuse to come away.)

I. Sop. THE MOTHERS
(with shrieks and threats) *deciso*

f Ah!
Ah!

and giving his orders in a loud voice)
MARCEL

turkey!
- chi-no!

SCHAUNARD

And some Rhenish!
Vin del Re-no!

And some lobster, on-ly
A-ra-go-sta sen-za

COLLINE

Bring some claret, too!
Vin da ta-vo-la!

13 *risoluto*

114

116

(Parpignol moves on, down the Rue Vieille Comédie, the children merrily follow him pretending to play on their toy instruments)

MIMI

like this but I could not,............... he quick -
co - sa de - si - a - ta................. ed e -

MIMI

rall.   stent.   a Tempo

- ly   found out   what my heart had   longed.......................
- gli ha   let - to   quel che il co - re a - scon - - -

a Tempo

rall.   stent.

MIMI

for;...........   Now one who
- de ....   O - ra co -

p

MIMI   rall.

reads the heart's long cher-ished   sec - rets   is   a
- lui che leg-ge den-tro a un   cuo - - re   sa   l'a -

rall.

(Enter from the corner of the Rue Mazarin an extremely pretty, coquettish-looking young lady.
She is followed by a pompous old gentleman who is both fussy and overdressed.)

RUDOLPH

Allegro moderato ♩.= 132

(surprised to see Musetta)

Oh!   Mu_set _ ta!
Oh!   *Mu_set _ ta!*

MARCEL   (throwing himself on a chair)

of   poison!   Herself!
tos _ si_co!   *Es_sa!*

SCHAUNARD   (in amazement)

Oh!   Mu_set _ ta!
Oh!   *Mu_set _ ta!*

COLLINE   (in amazement)

Oh!   Mu_set _ ta!
Oh!   *Mu_set _ ta!*

16   **Allegro moderato** ♩.= 132

ff brillante

SHOP-WOMEN.

Sop.ᴵ (perceiving Musetta)

Look!
To'!

Yes!
Sì!

She! Mu_set_ta!
Lei! Mu_set_ta!

Sop.ᴵ

She!
Lei!

Look!
to'!

Mu_set_ta!
Tor_na_ta!

subito pp

Oh! what swag-ger!
Sia_mo in au_ge!

My! she's gor_geous!
Che toe_let_ta!

(walking swiftly and looking about her, as if
in search of some one, while Alcindoro fol_
lows, panting and testy.)

ALCINDORO (breathless)

Just like a val___et
Come un fac-chi___no...

I must run here and there.
cor_rer di qua... di là...

p

p

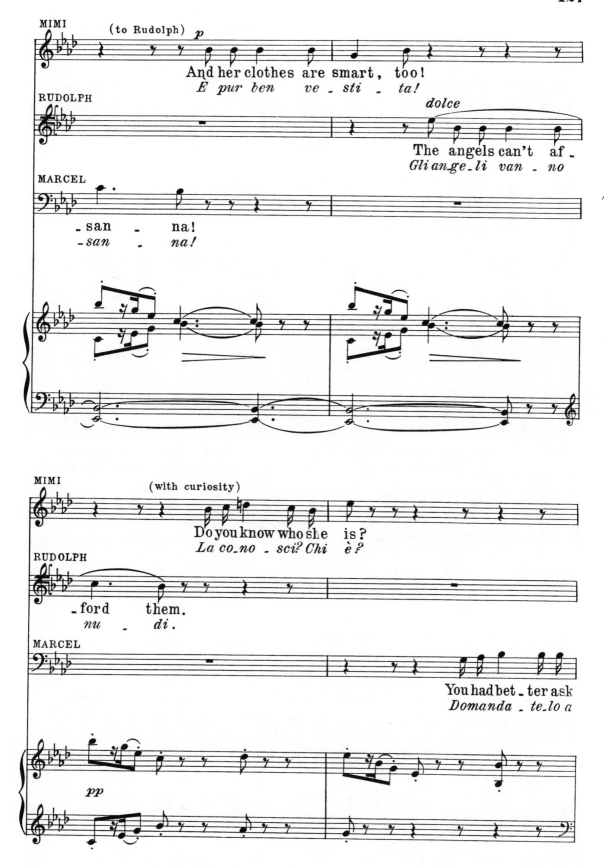

_set_ta!
_set_ta!
(they cross the stage)

yes! 'tis she, Mu_
pro _ prio lei, Mu_

Some old stamm'ring do _ tard's with her;yes! 'tis she, Mu_
Con quel vec _ chio che bal _ bet _ ta, pro _ prio lei, Mu_

_set_ta!   Ah! ah! ah! ah! ah! ah!   ah!
_set_ta!   Ah! ah! ah! ah! ah! ah!   ah!

(laughing)   leggerissimo

_set_ta!   Ah! ah! ah! ah! ah! ah!   ah!
_set_ta!   Ah! ah! ah! ah! ah! ah!   ah!

cres. poco a poco

MUSETTA

(Can he be jealous of this old mummy?   But
(Che sia ge_lo_so di que_sta mummia?   Ve_

ALCINDORO
(ceasing to give his orders and endeavouring

What strange be_
La con _ ve_

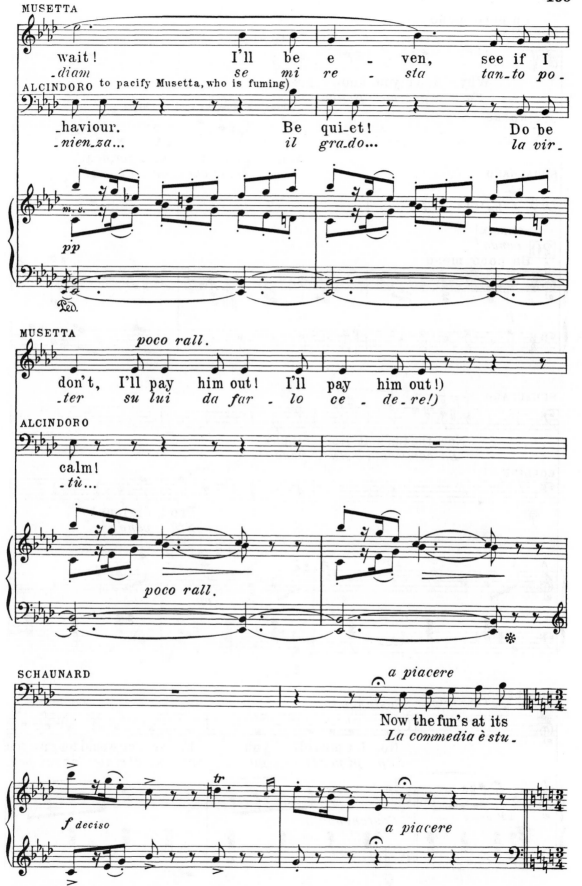

148

(pretending to suffer violent pain in her foot she sits down again)

MUSETTA *strillando, quasi a piacere*

(coyly showing her foot)
con grazia

Oh, dear! how it pains me! how it pains me! my foot!
Ahi! *sostenuto* *qual do_lo_re, qual bru_cio_re!* *Al piè!*

ALCINDORO

(bends down to untie her shoe)

What now? Let's see!
Che c'è? *Do_ve?*

col canto

MUSETTA

(screaming) **I.º Tempo**

Break it! tear it!
Sciogli, slac_cia,

MARCEL

(greatly concerned, comes forward)

Ah,
Gio'

a Tempo **I.º Tempo**

cres. molto

MUSETTA

I can't bear it! do, I beg you! Close by there is a
rompi, strac_cia! *te ne implo_ro...* *Laggiù c'è un calzo_*

MARCEL

gol _ den youth............you are not dead, not
_ven _ tù *mi _ a............tu non........* *se _ i*

quasi rit.
forte tutti

are empty; none can explain the sudden disappearance of Schaunard's purse; and they look at each other in surprise.)

MUSETTA   (to the waiter)

And my bill   please bring to
Il mio con _ to   da _ te a

STREET ARABS   (trying to get their bearings)

Will they come a_long this way?
S'av_vi _ ci_nan per di qua!?

MUSETTA

me.
me.

(pointing in an uncertain fashion the opposite way)

They are com_ing   down this way!
S'av_vi_ci_nan   per di là!

WORK-GIRLS
Sopr.

(Several windows are opened, at which mothers with their children appear
and eagerly await the coming of the Patrol.)

No. from there!
No, di là!

Ten. STUDENTS

No, from there!
No, di là!

160

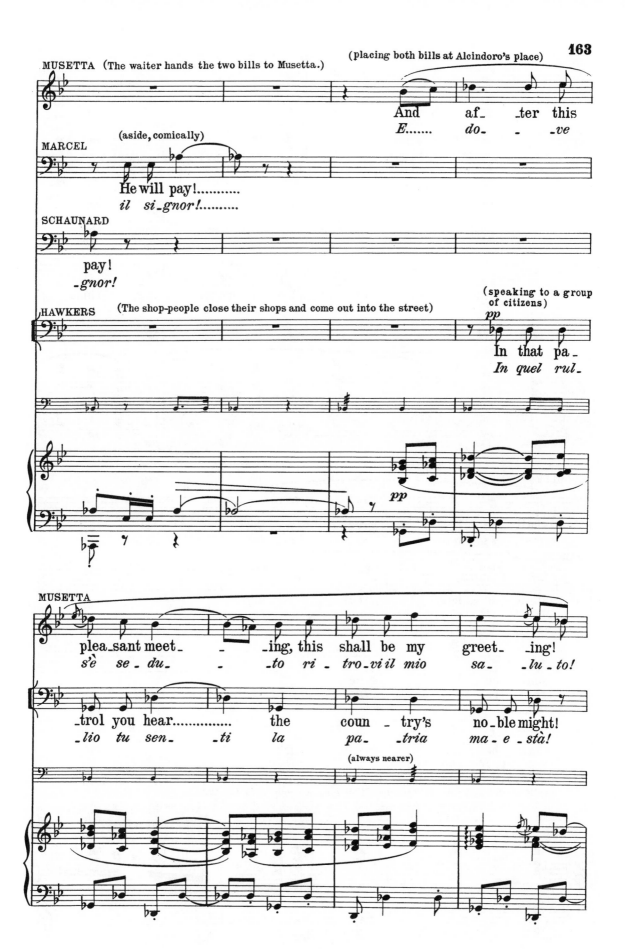

MUSETTA (The waiter hands the two bills to Musetta.) (placing both bills at Alcindoro's place)

And af_ _ter this
E....... do_ _ _ve

MARCEL (aside, comically)

He will pay!...........
il si_gnor!..........

SCHAUNARD

pay!
_gnor!

HAWKERS (The shop-people close their shops and come out into the street) (speaking to a group of citizens)
pp

In that pa_
In quel rul_

pp

MUSETTA

plea_sant meet_ _ _ing, this shall be my greet_ _ing!
s'è se_ du_ _ _to ri_ tro_vi il mio sa_ _lu_to!

trol you hear.............. the coun _try's no_ble might!
lio tu sen _ti la pa_ _tria ma_ e_ stà!

(always nearer)

(All look to the left; the tattoo is about to enter the square, when the crowd retreats on either side, while the friends with Musetta and Mimi form a group near the Café.)

(coming nearer and nearer)

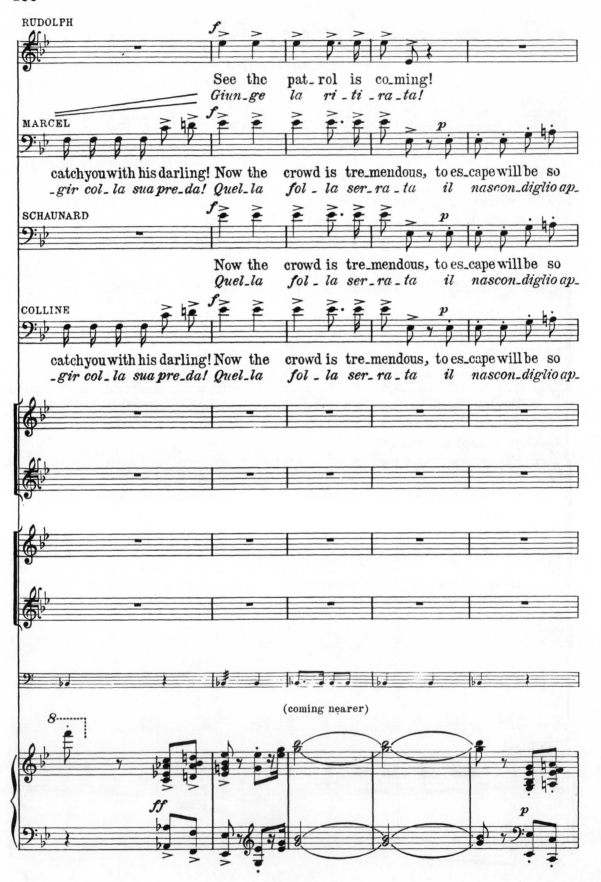

170

(The Tattoo crosses the scene, heading toward the right back)

Here come the sappers, look!........ There's the drum-ma-jor too!...........
I Zap-pa-to-ri o - là!........... Ec-co il tam-bur maggior!...........

Here come the sappers, look!........ There's the drum-ma-jor too!...........
I Zap-pa-to-ri o - là!........... Ec-co il tam-bur maggior!...........

Here come the sappers, look!........ There's the drum-ma-jor too!...........
I Zap-pa-to-ri o - là!........... Ec-co il tam-bur maggior!...........

Here come the sappers, look!........ There's the drum-ma-jor too!...........
I Zap-pa-to-ri o - là!........... Ec-co il tam-bur maggior!...........

Here come the sappers, look!........ There's the drum-ma-jor too!...........
I Zap-pa-to-ri o - là!........... Ec-co il tam-bur maggior!...........

Here come the sappers, look!........ There's the drum-ma-jor too!...........
I Zap-pa-to-ri o - là!........... Ec-co il tam-bur maggior!...........

(Musetta being without her shoe, cannot walk, so Marcel and Colline carry her through the crowd, as they endeavor to follow the
patrol. The mob, seeing her borne along in this triumphal fashion,
give her a regular ovation. Marcel and Colline with Musetta

See! there he goes. The tall drum-major bold!...... The
Ec _ co _ lo là! Il bel tam_bur maggior!... La

See! there he goes. The tall drum-major bold!....... The
Ec _ co _ lo là! Il bel tam_bur maggior!.... La

See! there he goes. The tall drum-major bold!...... The
Ec _ co _ lo là! Il bel tam_bur maggior!.... La

See! there he goes. The tall drum-major bold!...... The
Ec _ co _ lo là! Il bel tam_bur maggior!.... La

See! there he goes. The tall drum-major bold!...... The
Ec _ co _ lo là! Il bel tam_bur maggior!.... La

See! there he goes. The tall drum-major bold!..... The
Ec _ co _ lo là! Il bel tam_bur maggior!.... La

34

follow the patrol; Rudolph and Mimi follow arm in arm; Schaunard goes next, blowing his horn; while the students, work-girls,
street-lads, women and towns-folk merrily bring up the rear.

Marching in time with the music, the whole vast crowd gradually
moves off as it follows the patrol.)

(Meanwhile Alcindoro, with a pair of shoes carefully wrapped up, returns to the café in search of Musetta. The waiter by the table takes up the bill left by Mu_

RUDOLPH

_tin!
_tin!

setta and ceremoniously hands it to Alcindoro, who, seeing the amount, and per_ceiving that they have all left him there alone, falls back into a chair, utterly dumbfounded.)

MARCEL

_tin!
_tin!

SCHAUNARD

_tin!
_tin!

COLLINE

_tin!
_tin!

turns!
va!

turns!
va!

turns!
va!

turns!
va!

turns!
va!

turns!
va!

turns!
va!

En of Act. II.

THIRD
ACT

THIRD ACT

THE BARRIÈRE D'ENFER

Beyond the toll-gate, the outer boulevard is formed in the background by the Orleans high-road, half hidden by tall houses and the misty gloom of February.

To the left is a tavern with a small open space in front of the toll-gate. To the right is the Boulevard d'Enfer; to the left that of S.ᵗ Jacques.

On the right also there is the entrance to the Rue d'Enfer leading to the Quartier Latin.

Over the tavern, as its sign-board, hangs Marcel's picture "The Passage of the Red Sea," while under‐neath in large letters is the inscription "At the Port of Marseilles." On either side of the door are fres‐coes of a Turk and a Zouave with a huge laurel wreath round his fez.

From the ground-floor windows of the tavern facing the toll-gate, light gleams.

The plane-trees, grey and gaunt, which flank the toll-gate square lead diagonally towards the two boule‐vards. Between each tree is a marble bench. It is towards the close of February; snow covers all.

As the curtain rises the scene is merged in the dim light of early dawn.

In front of a brazier are seated, in a group, snoring custom-house officers. From the tavern at inter‐vals one may hear laughter, shouts, and the clink of glasses. A customhouse official comes out of the ta‐vern with wine. The toll-gate is closed.

(Behind the toll-gate, stamping their feet and blowing on their frost-bitten fingers, stand several street scavengers)

SCAVENGERS
8 Bassi

(vigorously) *mf*

What
Ohè,

(The officials do not budge; so the scavengers with brooms and mattocks thump the toll-gate and shout)

there!   What ho there!   Ad-mit us!
là,   le guardie!..   A-pri-te!..

182

(From the Tavern: The clink of glasses forms an accompaniment to the song)

3 Sop. 1.

3 Sop. 2.

3 Cont.

(from within)

dolce con grazia

Pass the glass! Let each toast his lass! So pass the glass! Let
Chi nel ber tro — vò il pia — cer, nel suo bic-chier, nel

each lad toast his lass! Ha!........................ Each one as he
su — o bic — chier, Aa!........................ d'u — na

sips, as he sips his wine, shall dream of lips made for love di -
boc — ca nel — l'ar — dor, tro — vò l'a — mor, tro — vò l'a —

CUSTOM-HOUSE OFFICIAL

(A sergeant comes out of the guard-house, and orders the toll-gate to be opened)

Here come the women with their milk!
Son già le lat_ti_ven_do_le!

6 MILK-WOMEN
Sop.
(from within) *f*
(*Exclaimed, not intoned*)

Houp-là! Houp-là!
Hopp_là! Hopp_là!

(a tinkling of carters' bells is heard)

ff subito pp

pp

3 CARTERS
(from within)
(*Exclaimed*)
(cracking of whips)

(Carts pass along the outer Boulevard, lighted by large lanterns)

Houp - là!
Hopp - là!

6 MILK-WOMEN
(quite close)
(*Exclaimed*)

(the gloom gradually gives way to daylight)

Houp - là!
Hopp - là!

mf pp

pp

(they move off in various directions)

la _ ter?
tar _ di?

At twelve o' _ clock!
A mez _ zo _ di!

At twelve o' _ clock!....
A mez _ zo _ di!........

(The officials remove

the bench and the brazier)

(Enter Mimi from the Rue d'Enfer: she looks about as if anxious to make sure of her whereabouts. On reaching the first plane-tree, she is seized by a violent fit of coughing. Then recovering herself, she sees the sergeant, whom she approaches)

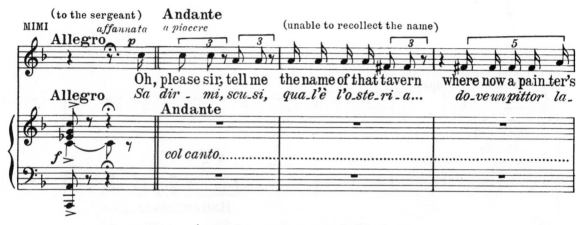

MIMI (to the sergeant) *affannata*

Oh, please sir, tell me the name of that tavern where now a pain_ter's
*Sa dir_mi, scu_si, qua_l'è l'o_ste_ri_a... do_ve un pittor la_*

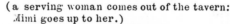

(a serving woman comes out of the tavern: Mimi goes up to her.)

MIMI (cough)

work_ing. Thank you. Oh! my good wo_man, pray do me this
*-vo_ra? Gra_zie. O buo_na don_na, mi fa_te il fa_*

SERGEANT (pointing to the cabaret)

There it is.
Ec_co_la.

MIMI

fa_vour! Can you find me the pain_ter, Mar_cel? I fain would
*-vo_re... di cer_car_mi il pit_to_re Mar_cel_lo? Ho da par_*

189

(Marcel goes towards Rudolph)

pp *mf* *f*

(coming out of the inn, hastens towards Marcel.)

RUDOLPH

Moderato con moto

Mar _ cel, at last I've found you!   Where none can
Mar _ cel _ lo. Fi _ nal _ men _ te!   *Qui niun ci*

Moderato con moto

RUDOLPH

a piacere

hear us.   I want a se _ par _ a _ tion from Mi _
sen _ te.   *Io voglio se _ pa _ rar _ mi da Mi _*

string.   *f col canto* ....

a Tempo

RUDOLPH

_ mi.
_ mì.

MARCEL

Is that your lat _ est whim?
Sei vo _ lu _ bil co _ sì?

a Tempo

ff   *f*   *leggero*

208

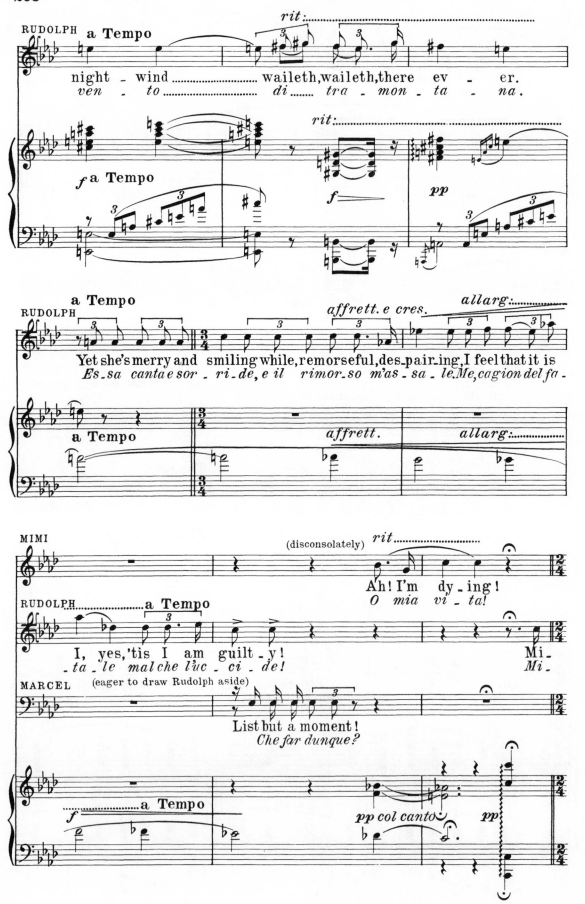

MIMI (Mimi's violent coughing and sobbing reveal her presence.)

rall:...................... a Tempo

gone;.......... and she must die!...
-tvs-   -ser fin-ti   fior!...

a Tempo

pp   *m.s.*

rall:...................   *rall.*

MIMI   Lento   *rall................And.*^no *mosso* ♩=84   *ritenuto*

Farewell, then,   I wish   you   well!..........   Nay, lis-ten,
Ad-di-o,   sen-za ran - cor............   A-scolta, a-

And.^no *mosso* ♩=84

27

col canto.................   *pp*   *p rit. col canto*

MIMI   a Tempo

lis - ten! Those things, those few old things I'- ve   left be-
-scol- ta.   Le po-che ro-be a-du-na che   la-sciai

a Tempo

pp

MIMI   3/4   5/4

-hind   me   With-in my trunk, safe are stor-ed
spar- se.   Nel mio cas-set-to stan chiu-si

pp leggerissimo   *pp leggero*

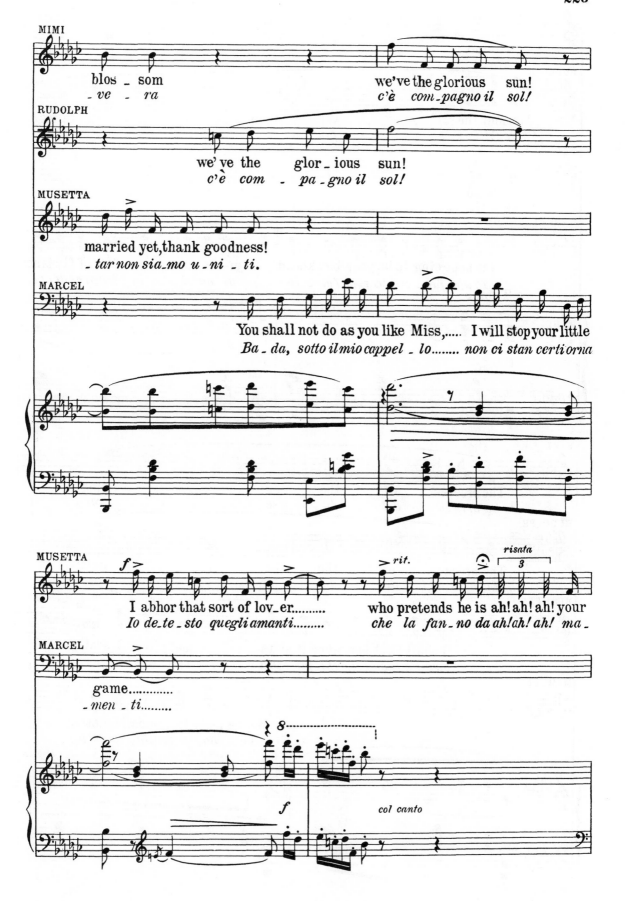

227

End of Act. III.

FOURTH
ACT

FOURTH ACT

IN THE ATTIC

(as in Act I.)

RUDOLPH (to Marcel, offering him some bread)

Choose, my lord mar _ quis, sal _ mon or
Scel _ gui o Ba _ ro _ ne tro _ ta o sal_

RUDOLPH

tur_bot?
-mo_ne?

(his offer is accepted, when turning to Schaunard, he proffers another crust of bread.)

MARCEL

Now duke, here's a
Du_ca, u _ na

MARCEL rit.   a Tempo

choice vol_au_vent with mushrooms!
lin_gua di pap _ pa _ gal _ lo?

Sostenendo un poco   **a Tempo**

SCHAUNARD (he politely declines and pours out a glass water which he hands to Marcel.) (the one and only

Thank you, I dare not! This evening, I'm dancing.
Gra_zie, m'in_pingua. Stas _ se _ra ho un bal_lo.

Sostenendo un poco

p stacc.

p

tumbler is handed about. Colline, after voraciously devouring his roll, rises.)

f

RUDOLPH

(to Colline)

What? sa_ted?
Già sa_zio?

p

COLLINE   (with an air of grave importance.)

To business!   The king a _ waits me!
Ho fretta.   *Il Re m'a _ spetta.*

he takes up the water-bottle and goes out after Colline, gently closing the door.)

cres. e affrett.

pp

rall.

21 Più sostenuto

(Mimi opens her eyes and, seeing that all have gone, holds out her hand to Rudolph who affectio-

pp dolciss.

cres.

pp

_nately kisses it)

MIMI

con grande espress.

Have they
So - no an -

rall:.................

MIMI And.^{te} calmo (Rudolph nods)

left us? To sleep I on-ly feign-ed,..... for I want-ed to be a-lone with
-da - ti? Fin-ge-vo di dor-mi - re...... per-chè vol-li con te so-la re-

MIMI

you, love.... So ma-ny things there are that I would tell you; there is
-sta - re...... Ho tan-te co - se che ti vo-glio di - re....... o u-na

MIMI   (raising herself somewhat, with Rudolph's help)

one too, as spacious as the o-cean,... as the o-cean pro-found, with-out
so - la, ma grande co-me il ma - re,..... co-me il ma - re profonda ed in - fi-

cres.

MIMI   con espansione   (putting her arms round Rudolph's neck)   poco rit.
                                                                            p dolcissimo

lim-it........ ah! my love,... you are my on-ly love, You are my
-ni - ta........ Sei il mio a-mor..... e tut-ta la mia vi-ta, Sei il mio a-

f

p poco rit.

MIMI

poco rall:.................   *molto rall.*   *Più Sostenuto*

fair as the flame of sun - set.   "They call........
bel - la co - me un tra - mon - to.   *«Mi chia - ma -*

MIMI   *(like an echo)*   *molto rall:.........*

me Mi - mi,..............   they call........   me Mi -
- no Mi - mi,..............   *mi chia - ma - no Mi -*

MIMI

- mi.................. but I know   not why.".
- mì..................   *il per - chè....*   *non so...»*

23

All^{tto} mosso

RUDOLPH (in tender, caressing tones)   (he takes out the

Back to her nest comes the swal-low in the spring-tide
Tor - nò al ni - do la ron - di - ne e cin - guet - ta.

MIMI

And you, my young mas — ter, now I can tell you frankly
Mio bel si – gno – ri – no, pos – so ben dirlo a – des-so,

MIMI

that you soon man — aged to find it
lei la tro – vò as – sai pre – sto

MIMI

RUDOLPH

It was
E – ra

It was Fate that did help me
A – iu – ta – vo il de – sti – no

MIMI

(remembering her first meeting with Rudolph on Christmas Eve)

dark, and my blush — es were un — noticed "Your
buio, e il mio ros – sor non si ve – de – va *Che*

(Meanwhile Musetta is busily heating the medicine brought by Marcel over the spirit-lamp, as
she unconsciously murmurs a prayer.)

MUSETTA And.^{te} lento e sost.^{to}

Oh Ma_ry, blessed
*Madonna be_ne_*

RUDOLPH

(reassured at seeing Mimi fall asleep, he gently
moves away from the bedside and motioning the
others not to make any noise, he approaches Marcel)
pp sottovoce

What said the   doctor?
Che ha detto il   me_di_co?   *pp sottovoce*

MARCEL

29 And.^{te} lento e sost.^{to}

He'll come.
Ver_rà.

sf

(Rudolph, Marcel and Schaunard whisper together
Every now and then Rudolph goes on tip-toe to the
bed and then rejoins his companions)
MUSETTA

Virgin, save, of thy mer_cy this poor maiden, save her, Madon_na mine, from
*_det_ta, fa_te la grazia a questa po_ve_ret_ta che non deb_ba mo_*
dolce

pp   *pp*   *m.s.*

(interrupting, she bids Marcel place a book upright on the table, so as to shade the lamp.)
MUSETTA *quasi a piacere*..

death! Here there should be a shade,   because the lamp is flick_er_ing.   Like
*_ri_re. Qui ci   vuo_leun ri_pa_ro perchè la fiamma sven_to_la.   Co_*

col canto.............................

ppp
m.d.

MUSETTA (resuming her prayer)   a Tempo

this... And oh! may she re - cov - er,   Madon - na, Ho - ly Mother, I
_sì... E che pos - sa gua - ri - re.   Madon - na san - ta, io sono in -

pp

MUSETTA

me - rit not thy par - don, but our lit - tle Mi - mi's an an - gel from
_de - gna di per - do - no, mentre in - ve - ce Mi - mì è un an - ge - lo del

m.s.

MUSETTA   *rall:....................*

heaven!   Not serious.
cielo.   Non credo.

RUDOLPH (approaches Musetta while Schaunard advances on tip-toe to the bedside. With a sorrowful gesture he goes back to Marcel) *sottovoce*

I still have hope.   Do you think it is   serious? *(in a hoarse voice)*
Io spero an - co - ra. Vi pa - re che sia   grave?

SCHAUNARD   *p*

Marcel, she is
Marcello, è spi -

pppp   *rall:....................*

(unable to bear up any longer, he hastens to embrace Rudolph, as he murmurs:)

MARCEL **Largo sostenuto** *con angoscia*

Poor fel - low!
Co - rag - gio...

31

(flings himself on Mimi's bed,
lifts her up, shakes her by the
hand, and exclaims in tones of
RUDOLPH anguish)

(falls, sobbing, upon her
lifeless form)

Mimi!......
Mimi!.....

Mimi!..........
Mimi!..........

(Terrorstruck, Musetta rushes to the bed; utters a piercing cry of grief; then kneels sobbing at the foot
of the bed. Schaunard, overcome, sinks back into a chair, to the left. Colline stands at the foot of the
bed, dazed at the suddenness of this catastrophe.   Marcel, sobbing, turns his back to the foot_
_lights.)

(the curtain slowly falls)

Grave

The End.